foundations

SMALL GROUP STUDY GUIDE

taught by tom Holladay and kay warren

THE CHURCH

ZONDERVAN®

SADDLEBACK CHURCH

ZONDERVAN.com/
AUTHORTRACKER
follow your favorite authors

 ZONDERVAN®

Foundations: *The Church Study Guide*
Copyright © 2003, 2004, 2008 by Tom Holladay and Kay Warren

Requests for information should be addressed to:
Zondervan, *Grand Rapids, Michigan 49530*

ISBN 978-0-310-27692-0

08 09 10 11 12 13 14 15 16 17 18 • 23 22 21 20 19 18 17 16 15 14 13 12 11 10 9 8 7 6 5 4 3 2 1

FOREWORD

What *Foundations* Will Do for You

I once built a log cabin in the Sierra Mountains of northern California. After ten backbreaking weeks of clearing forest land, all I had to show for my effort was a leveled and squared concrete foundation. I was discouraged, but my father, who built over a hundred church buildings in his lifetime, said, "Cheer up, son! Once you've laid the foundation, the most important work is behind you." I've since learned that this is a principle for all of life: you can never build *anything* larger than the foundation can handle.

The foundation of any building determines both its size and strength, and the same is true of our lives. A life built on a false or faulty foundation will never reach the height that God intends for it to reach. If you skimp on your foundation, you limit your life.

That's why this material is so vitally important. *Foundations* is the biblical basis of a purpose-driven life. You must understand these life-changing truths to enjoy God's purposes for you. This curriculum has been taught, tested, and refined over ten years with thousands of people at Saddleback Church. I've often said that *Foundations* is the most important class in our church.

Why You Need a Biblical Foundation for Life

- *It's the source of personal growth and stability.* So many of the problems in our lives are caused by faulty thinking. That's why Jesus said the truth will set us free and why Colossians 2:7a (CEV) says, *"Plant your roots in Christ and let him be the foundation for your life."*

- *It's the underpinning of a healthy family.* Proverbs 24:3 (TEV) says, *"Homes are built on the foundation of wisdom and understanding."* In a world that is constantly changing, strong families are based on God's unchanging truth.

- **It's the starting point of leadership.** You can never lead people farther than you've gone yourself. Proverbs 16:12b (MSG) says, *"Sound leadership has a moral foundation."*

- **It's the basis for your eternal reward in heaven.** Paul said, *"Whatever we build on that foundation will be tested by fire on the day of judgment . . . We will be rewarded if our building is left standing"* (1 Corinthians 3:12, 14 CEV).

- **God's truth is the only foundation that will last.** The Bible tells us that *"the sound, wholesome teachings of the Lord Jesus Christ . . . are the foundation for a godly life"* (1 Timothy 6:3 NLT), and that *"God's truth stands firm like a foundation stone . . ."* (2 Timothy 2:19 NLT).

Jesus concluded his Sermon on the Mount with a story illustrating this important truth. Two houses were built on different foundations. The house built on sand was destroyed when rain, floods, and wind swept it away. But the house built on the foundation of solid rock remained firm. He concluded, *"Therefore everyone who hears these words of mine and puts them into practice is like a wise man who built his house on the rock"* (Matthew 7:24 NIV). *The Message* paraphrase of this verse shows how important this is: *"These words I speak to you are not incidental additions to your life . . . They are foundational words, words to build a life on."*

I cannot recommend this curriculum more highly to you. It has changed our church, our staff, and thousands of lives. For too long, too many have thought of theology as something that doesn't relate to our everyday lives, but *Foundations* explodes that mold. This study makes it clear that the foundation of what we do and say in each day of our lives is what we believe. I am thrilled that this in-depth, life-changing curriculum is now being made available for everyone to use.

— Rick Warren, author of *The Purpose Driven® Life*

PREFACE

Get ready for a radical statement, a pronouncement sure to make you wonder if we've lost our grip on reality: *There is nothing more exciting than doctrine!*

Track with us for a second on this. Doctrine is the study of what God has to say. What God has to say is always the truth. The truth gives me the right perspective on myself and on the world around me. The right perspective results in decisions of faith and experiences of joy. *That* is exciting!

The objective of *Foundations* is to present the basic truths of the Christian faith in a simple, systematic, and life-changing way—in other words, to teach doctrine. The question is, why? In a world in which people's lives are filled with crying needs, why teach doctrine? Because biblical doctrine has the answer to many of those crying needs! Please don't see this as a clash between needs-oriented and doctrine-oriented teaching. The truth is we need both. We all need to learn how to deal with worry in our lives. One of the keys to dealing with worry is an understanding of the biblical doctrine of the hope of heaven. Couples need to know what the Bible says about how to have a better marriage. They also need a deeper understanding of the doctrine of the Fatherhood of God, giving the assurance of God's love upon which all healthy relationships are built. Parents need to understand the Bible's practical insights for raising kids. They also need an understanding of the sovereignty of God, a certainty of the fact that God is in control, that will carry them through the inevitable ups and downs of being a parent. Doctrinal truth meets our deepest needs.

Welcome to a study that will have a lifelong impact on the way you look at everything around you and above you and within you. Helping you develop a "Christian worldview" is our goal as the writers of this study. A Christian worldview is the ability to see everything through the filter of God's truth. The time you dedicate to this study will lay a foundation for new perspectives that will have tremendous benefits for the rest of your life. This study will help you:

- Lessen the stress in everyday life
- See the real potential for growth the Lord has given you
- Increase your sense of security in an often troubling world
- Find new tools for helping others (your friends, your family, your children) find the right perspective on life
- Fall more deeply in love with the Lord

Throughout this study you'll see four types of sidebar sections designed to help you connect with the truths God tells us about himself, ourselves, and this world.

- *A Closer Look:* We'll take time to expand on a truth or look at it from a different perspective.

- *A Fresh Word:* One aspect of doctrine that makes people nervous is the "big words." Throughout this study we'll take a fresh look at these words, words like *omnipotent* and *sovereign*.

- *Key Personal Perspective:* The truth of doctrine always has a profound impact on our lives. In this section we'll focus on that personal impact.

- *Living on Purpose:* James 1:22 (NCV) says, *"Do what God's teaching says; when you only listen and do nothing, you are fooling yourselves."* In his book, *The Purpose Driven Life,* Rick Warren identifies God's five purposes for our lives. They are worship, fellowship, discipleship, ministry, and evangelism. We will focus on one of these five purposes in each lesson, and discuss how it relates to the subject of the study. This section is very important, so please be sure to leave time for it.

Here is a brief explanation of the other features of this study guide.

Looking Ahead/Catching Up: You will open each meeting with an opportunity for everyone to check in with each other about how you are doing with the weekly assignments. Accountability is a key to success in this study!

Key Verse: Each week you will find a key verse or Scripture passage for your group to read together. If someone in the group has a different translation, ask them to read it aloud so the group can get a bigger picture of the meaning of the passage.

Video Lesson: There is a video lesson segment for the group to watch together each week. Take notes in the lesson outlines as you watch the video, and be sure to refer back to these notes during your discussion time.

Discovery Questions: Each video segment is complemented by questions for group discussion. Please don't feel pressured to discuss every single question. The material in this study is meant to be your servant, not your master, so there is no reason to rush through the answers. Give everyone ample opportunity to share their thoughts. If you don't get through all of the discovery questions, that's okay.

Prayer Direction: At the end of each session you will find suggestions for your group prayer time. Praying together is one of the greatest privileges of small group life. Please don't take it for granted.

Get ready for God to do incredible things in your life as you begin the adventure of learning more deeply about the most exciting message in the world: the truth about God!

— Tom Holladay and Kay Warren

HOW TO USE THIS VIDEO CURRICULUM

Here is a brief explanation of the features on your small group DVD. These features include a *Group Lifter*, four *Video Teaching Sessions* by Tom Holladay and Kay Warren and a short video, *How to Become a Follower of Jesus Christ*, by Rick Warren. Here's how they work:

The Group Lifter is a brief video introduction by Tom Holladay giving you a sense of the objectives and purpose of this *Foundations* study on the church. Watch it together as a group at the beginning of your first session.

The Video Teaching Sessions provide you with the teaching for each week of the study. Watch these features with your group. After watching the video teaching session, continue in your study by working through the discussion questions and activities in the study guide.

Nothing is more important than the decision you make to accept Jesus Christ as your Lord and Savior. You will have the option to watch a short video presentation, *How to Become a Follower of Jesus Christ*, at the end of Session One. In this brief video segment, Rick Warren explains the importance of having Christ as the Savior of your life and how you can become part of the family of God. If everyone in your group is already a follower of Christ, or if you feel there is a better time to play this segment, continue your session by turning to the Discovery Questions in your DVD study guide. You can also select this video presentation separately on the Main Menu of the DVD for viewing at any time.

Follow these simple steps for a successful small group session:

1. Hosts: Watch the video session and write down your answers to the discussion questions in the study guide before your group arrives.

2. Group: Open your group meeting by using the "Looking Ahead" or "Catching Up" section of your lesson.

3. Group: Watch the video teaching lesson and follow along in the outlines in the study guide.

4. Group: Complete the rest of the discussion materials for each session in the study guide.

It's just that simple. Have a great study together!

1

Session One

HOW THE CHURCH BEGAN

LOOKING AHEAD

1. What do you hope to get out of this small group study?

2. What picture comes to mind when you hear the word *church*?

Key Verse

"And I tell you that you are Peter, and on this rock I will build my church, and the gates of Hades will not overcome it."

Matthew 16:18 (NIV)

HOW THE CHURCH BEGAN

BIBLE TEACHING
Watch the video lesson now and take notes in
your outline on pages 3–6.

Have you ever heard someone ask, "Why is the church so important?
Why can't I just have a relationship with Jesus and forget about the
church?" We all know people who consider themselves Christians but
seldom attend church. Is the church really necessary? Absolutely! To
have faith in God means we cannot live the Christian life in isolation.
The truth is, we cannot live out the Christian life without belonging to
the church.

Our Need for the Church

God's Ideal	Our Actual Practice
Church is a spiritual necessity	Church is an optional activity
Interdependence is valued	Individualism is valued
Spirituality takes place in community	Religion is a private matter
Active involvement in social concerns	Aloof from the real world
All people fully accepted together (regardless of race, social status, etc.)	Segregation practiced
Authentic behavior, with the public and private lives matching	Hypocrisy; saying one thing but practicing another

The Beginning of the Church

1. _____ by God

> *For you are a people holy to the L*ORD *your God. The L*ORD *your God has chosen you out of all the peoples on the face of the earth to be his people, his treasured possession.* (Deuteronomy 7:6 NIV)

> *But you are a chosen people, a royal priesthood, a holy nation, a people belonging to God, that you may declare the praises of him who called you out of darkness into his wonderful light.* (1 Peter 2:9 NIV)

2. _____ by Jesus

> *". . . I will build my church; and the gates of hell shall not prevail against it."* (Matthew 16:18 KJV)

3. _____ by the Spirit

> *For we were all baptized by one Spirit into one body—whether Jews or Greeks, slave or free—and we were all given the one Spirit to drink.* (1 Corinthians 12:13 NIV)

The Nature of the Church
(What is the church supposed to be?)

The church is an _____ .

Ekklesia refers to both the _____ church and the _____ church.

- In the universal church the emphasis is on the _____ of the church.

- In the local church the emphasis is on the _____ of the church.

The church is a _____ .

A FRESH WORD
Koinonia

Another important Greek word that relates to the church is *koinonia*. While it is difficult to translate into English, it carries the idea of communion, fellowship, sharing, and participation. It is used to describe the life that the *ekklesia*, or church, is to share in Christ—our participation together in the life of God through Jesus Christ. Koinonia is a oneness that is only possible through God's supernatural work.

Seven characteristics of koinonia:

1. _____ (1 John 1:6–7)

2. _____ (Philippians 2:1–2)

3. _____ (Philemon 1:17)

4. _____ (Acts 2:44–45)

5. _____ (2 Corinthians 8:4)

6. _____ (Philippians 3:8–10)

7. _____ (1 Corinthians 10:16)

A CLOSER LOOK
The Ordinances of the Church

The word *ordinance* comes from the word *ordained.* It refers to the events that Jesus specifically ordered us to make a regular part of our worship as a church. The two ordinances that Jesus gave to the church are baptism and the Lord's Supper.

1. Baptism demonstrates physically what took place spiritually when we accepted Christ. Through baptism, our participation in his death, burial, and resurrection is portrayed, and we rise up out of the water, symbolizing the new life we now have in Christ.

   Why is it important for you to be baptized as a believer in Christ? First and foremost, because Jesus commanded it! He ordained—he commanded—baptism to be a step we take as we follow him. In his Great Commission Jesus told us to *". . . make disciples of all nations, baptizing them in the name of the Father and of the Son and of the Holy Spirit."* (Matthew 28:19-20 NIV)

   When you are baptized, you are picturing to the world what happened in your life when you became a believer.

   We were therefore buried with him through baptism into death in order that, just as Christ was raised from the dead through the glory of the Father, we too may live a new life. (Romans 6:4 NIV)

2. The Lord's Supper, or Communion, also is a physical reminder of deep, spiritual realities. We remember that through his broken body and spilled blood a new covenant has been established between God and man.

   [24]and when he had given thanks, he broke it and said, "This is my body, which is for you; do this in remembrance of me." [25]In the same way, after supper he took the cup, saying, "This cup is the new covenant in my blood; do this, whenever you drink it, in remembrance of me." [26]For whenever you eat this bread and drink this cup, you proclaim the Lord's death until he comes. (1 Corinthians 11:24-26 NIV)

Sometimes the ordinances are called *sacraments*, from the Latin *Sacramentum*, which was an oath of allegiance a Roman soldier took to his emperor. Christians took over the term and meant that it bound them in loyalty to Christ. In the ordinances, Christ's grace and forgiveness are depicted—they are sermons acted out. We are allowed the opportunity to express our allegiance and loyalty to Christ when we are baptized and when we eat the Lord's Supper together. The ordinances do not give us more of God's grace. They are a way to praise God for the grace we've already received.

DISCOVERY QUESTIONS

1. Why is it important for individual believers to be involved consistently with a body of believers? How would you respond to someone who tells you they don't need to belong to a church or that they don't need fellowship?

2. Look back at the chart "Our Need for the Church" on page 3. Which of the contrasts between God's Ideal and Our Actual Practice do you see as your greatest challenge? Why?

Did You Get It? How has this week's study helped you to see the meaning of fellowship in new or deeper ways?

Share with Someone: Think of a person you can encourage with the truth you learned in this session. Write their name in the space below and pray for God to provide that opportunity this week.

LIVING ON PURPOSE
Fellowship

Look again at the word study on *koinonia* and the seven characteristics which describe *koinonia* fellowship. Which of these is most important to you personally? Which characteristics are strengths for your group? In which characteristics do you as a group desire to grow? How can you live on purpose regarding *koinonia* fellowship in your small group this next week?

PRAYER DIRECTION

Take some time as a group to talk about your specific prayer requests and to pray for one another. Thank God for the "church" that is here in this room right now.

"HOW TO BECOME A FOLLOWER OF JESUS CHRIST"

Have you ever surrendered your life to Jesus Christ? Take a few minutes with your group to watch a brief video by Pastor Rick Warren on how to become part of the family of God. It is included on the Main Menu of this DVD.

Session two

2

THE PURPOSE OF
THE CHURCH

CATCHING UP

1. Who did you share last week's truth with?

2. Discuss last week's "Living on Purpose" activity. How did you see the fellowship that is to be ours in the church expressed through your group this last week?

Key Verse

Let us not give up meeting together, as some are in the habit of doing, but let us encourage one another—and all the more as you see the Day approaching.

Hebrews 10:25 (NIV)

BIBLE TEACHING
Watch the video lesson now and take notes in your outline on pages 11–12.

The Mission of the Church
(What is the church supposed to do?)

The Five Purposes of the Church

The five purposes of the church are given in two statements of Jesus: the Great Commandment and the Great Commission.

The Great Commandment

> [37]Jesus replied: "'Love the Lord your God with all your heart and with all your soul and with all your mind.' [38]This is the first and greatest commandment. [39]And the second is like it: 'Love your neighbor as yourself.' [40]All the Law and the Prophets hang on these two commandments."
> (Matthew 22:37–40 NIV)

The Great Commission

> [19]"Therefore go and make disciples of all nations, baptizing them in the name of the Father and of the Son and of the Holy Spirit, [20]and teaching them to obey everything I have commanded you. And surely I am with you always, to the very end of the age." (Matthew 28:19–20 NIV)

Instructions for the church

1. "Love God with all your heart": _____

2. "Love your neighbor as yourself": _____

3. "Go and make disciples": _____

4. "Baptizing them": _____

5. "Teaching them to do": _____

The church exists to:

1. Celebrate God's _____ (worship)

> *O magnify the LORD with me, and let us exalt his name together!* (Psalm 34:3 RSV)

2. Communicate God's _____ (evangelism)

> *The most important thing is that I complete my mission, the work that the Lord Jesus gave me—to tell people the Good News about God's grace.* (Acts 20:24 NCV)

3. Incorporate God's _____ (fellowship)

> *. . . you are members of God's very own family . . . and you belong in God's household with every other Christian.* (Ephesians 2:19 LB)

4. Educate God's _____ (discipleship)

> *[12]. . . building up the church, the body of Christ, to a position of strength and maturity; [13]until . . . all become full-grown in the Lord . . .* (Ephesians 4:12–13 LB)

5. Demonstrate God's _____ (ministry)

> *To equip the saints for the work of ministry . . .* (Ephesians 4:12 NRSV)

DISCOVERY QUESTIONS

1. God clearly tells us there are five purposes for the church and each is important. Which purposes come easily for you and which are more difficult? How have you experienced growth in any of the purposes over the past year?

2. How could you, as a small group, help each other with your next step of spiritual growth? Is it becoming a member of a church? Is it completing a church membership class? Is it developing a plan for healthy spiritual growth? Is it asking someone to be your spiritual partner? Is it getting involved in ministry? Is it learning to share your faith? What opportunities are available at your church to help you grow in each of the purposes? How are you currently taking advantage of opportunities for growth?

Did You Get It? How has this week's study helped you gain new insight into your part in the mission of the church?

Share with Someone: Think of a person you can encourage with the truth you learned in this session. Write their name in the space below and pray for God to provide that opportunity this week.

LIVING ON PURPOSE
Fellowship

This week, memorize your church's purpose statement and think through each aspect of it. Consider how you are doing at living it out. Ask God to show you what you can do to improve in areas where you are weak. If your church does not have a purpose statement, use the following purpose statement of Saddleback Church as an example:

> #### PURPOSE STATEMENT OF THE CHURCH
> To bring people to Jesus and to membership in his family, to develop them to Christlike maturity, and to equip them for their ministry in the church and their life mission in the world in order to magnify God's name.

PRAYER DIRECTION

During your group prayer time, pray for churches other than your own. Pray for churches of family and friends. Pray for churches you may have belonged to in the past. Pray for other churches in your community. (In week four, we will pray for churches in other countries.)

3

Session three

METAPHORS FOR
THE CHURCH

CATCHING UP

1. Share a step you took this past week to grow in one of the five purposes of the church.

2. What did you learn through memorizing your church's purpose statement?

Key Verse

Now you are no longer strangers to God and foreigners to heaven,
but you are members of God's very own family, citizens of God's country,
and you belong in God's household with every other Christian.

Ephesians 2:19 (LB)

BIBLE TEACHING
Watch the video lesson now and take notes in your outline on pages 17–19.

The Metaphors for the Church

The _____ of Christ

The church is Jesus' body and Jesus is the head of the body.

> *²²And God placed all things under his feet and appointed him to be head over everything for the church, ²³which is his body, the fullness of him who fills everything in every way.* (Ephesians 1:22–23 NIV)

Two words are crucial as we study the body of Christ:

1) _____

2) _____

Our unity

> *¹⁴For Christ himself is our way of peace. He has made peace between us Jews and you Gentiles by making us all one family, breaking down the wall of contempt that used to separate us. ¹⁵By his death he ended the angry resentment between us, caused by the Jewish laws which favored the Jews and excluded the Gentiles, for he died to annul that whole system of Jewish laws. Then he took the two groups that had been opposed to each other and made them parts of himself; thus he fused us together to become one new person, and at last there was peace. ¹⁶As parts of the same body, our anger against each other has disappeared, for both of us have been reconciled to God. And so the feud ended at last at the cross. ¹⁹Now you are no longer strangers to God and foreigners to heaven, but*

you are members of God's very own family, citizens of God's country, and you belong in God's household with every other Christian. (Ephesians 2:14–16, 19 LB)

- Christ breaking down the wall of _____ (v. 14)
- Our _____ in Christ's body (v. 15)
- Our _____ at the cross (v. 16)
- A common _____ , a common _____ , and a common _____ destination (v. 19)

KEY PERSONAL PERSPECTIVE
How Do I Handle a Disagreement with a Fellow Believer?

The wrong way: _____

   . . . *gossip separates the best of friends.* (Proverbs 16:28 NLT)

The right way: _____ it

[15]"If another believer sins against you, go privately and point out the fault. If the other person listens and confesses it, you have won that person back. [16]But if you are unsuccessful, take one or two others with you and go back again, so that everything you say may be confirmed by two or three witnesses. [17]If that person still refuses to listen, take your case to the church. If the church decides you are right, but the other person won't accept it, treat that person as a pagan or a corrupt tax collector." (Matthew 18:15–17 NLT)

[23]"Therefore, if you are offering your gift at the altar and there remember that your brother has something against you, [24]leave your gift there in front of the altar. First go and be reconciled to your brother; then come and offer your gift." (Matthew 5:23–24 NIV)

Our diversity

[14]Now the body is not made up of one part but of many. [15]If the foot should say, "Because I am not a hand, I do not belong to the body," it would not for that reason cease to be part of the body. [16]And if the ear should say, "Because I am not an eye, I

do not belong to the body," it would not for that reason cease to be part of the body. [17]If the whole body were an eye, where would the sense of hearing be? If the whole body were an ear, where would the sense of smell be?
(1 Corinthians 12:14–17 NIV)

[4]Just as each of us has one body with many members, and these members do not all have the same function, [5]so in Christ we who are many form one body, and each member belongs to all the others. (Romans 12:4–5 NIV)

The _____ of God

"I have other sheep that are not of this sheep pen. I must bring them also. They too will listen to my voice, and there shall be one flock and one shepherd." (John 10:16 NIV)

- We are the _____.

This image emphasizes that members of the church, as the sheep of Christ, belong to him.

[26]"But you do not believe because you are not my sheep. [27]My sheep listen to my voice; I know them, and they follow me. [28]I give them eternal life, and they shall never perish; no one can snatch them out of my hand. [29]My Father, who has given them to me, is greater than all; no one can snatch them out of my Father's hand." (John 10:26–29 NIV)

- Jesus is the _____.

This metaphor of Jesus as our shepherd shows his love and care for us.

[11]"I am the good shepherd. The good shepherd lays down his life for the sheep. [14]I am the good shepherd; I know my sheep and my sheep know me—[15]just as the Father knows me and I know the Father—and I lay down my life for the sheep. [16]I have other sheep that are not of this sheep pen. I must bring them also. They too will listen to my voice, and there shall be one flock and one shepherd." (John 10:11, 14–16 NIV)

DISCOVERY QUESTIONS

1. How do our relationships with other believers bring authenticity to our Christian life?

2. *The church is the body of Christ.* Every part of the body is important. Do you feel like you're an important part of the body of Christ? What would help you see your role in the church as vital?

3. What difference would it make if everyone in a church or small group used his or her gifts to benefit the body? What would be lost if even one person in your small group didn't use his or her gifts for the good of the body of Christ? How can you effectively encourage one another to use your gifts?

4. *The church is the flock of God.* What did you learn about Jesus from the metaphor of the shepherd? What did you learn about yourself from the metaphor of sheep? As one of his flock, how have you experienced Jesus being your shepherd?

5. Why is gossip so destructive? What are some subtle ways we tend to discuss things that in the end are nothing but gossip? Is this an issue in your group? If so, how can you commit and work together to keep it from happening?

6. How is a diversity of gifts and personalities important to your small group? What can you do to embrace your diversity and still maintain your unity?

Did You Get It? How has this week's study helped you see the significance and personal meaning of the church as the body of Christ and the flock of God?

Share with Someone: Think of a person you can encourage with the truth you learned in this session. Write their name in the space below and pray for God to provide that opportunity this week.

LIVING ON PURPOSE
Fellowship

How do you handle problems with other believers? Is there anyone in your life right now with whom you need to resolve a problem? Do you have something against another, or does someone have something against you? If so, take steps this week to bring about reconciliation. Make an appointment to go to that someone and offer forgiveness or seek forgiveness. This may be the most difficult purpose activity in the entire Foundations series—yet it promises dramatic change in your life and lasting glory for God.

PRAYER DIRECTION

Take some time as a group to talk about your specific prayer requests and to pray for one another. Thank God for the importance of each group member to the body of Christ.

Preparation for Next Time:

1. For next week's "Living on Purpose" activity, you will share the Lord's Supper together as a group. The Lord's Supper is an expression of participating in the life and death of Jesus Christ. When we share this experience together we worship our Lord for coming, dying, and providing the opportunity for eternal life. Take a few moments now to plan this time of communion. Turn to pages 49–50 in the Small Group Resources section for instructions.

2. Bring a family photo to your next meeting. This can be a picture from a vacation, family gathering, holiday, or a portrait of a special time or season of your family.

   At the next session, plan to take a group photo and start your own small group family album.

NOTES

Session four

4

METAPHORS FOR
THE CHURCH—PART 2

CATCHING UP

1. Who did you share last week's truth with?

2. Discuss last week's "Living on Purpose" activity. If any of you took steps toward reconciling a broken relationship, share how it went.

3. Show your family photos to each other and explain the special moments they represent. Take a picture of your small group family and ask someone in the group to begin creating a small group family album.

Key Verse

For we were all baptized by one Spirit into one body—whether Jews or Greeks, slave or free—and we were all given the one Spirit to drink.

1 Corinthians 12:13 (NIV)

BIBLE TEACHING
Watch the video lesson now and take notes in
your outline on pages 27–30.

The Metaphors of the Church (continued)

The _____ *(household) of God*

- God _____ us into his family.

    *For we were all baptized by one Spirit into one body—whether
    Jews or Greeks, slave or free—and we were all given the one
    Spirit to drink.* (1 Corinthians 12:13 NIV)

    *And so we should not be like cringing, fearful slaves, but we
    should behave like God's very own children, adopted into
    the bosom of his family, and calling to him, "Father, Father."*
    (Romans 8:15 LB)

- We're to _____ one another as family.

    *[1]Do not rebuke an older man harshly, but exhort him as if he
    were your father. Treat younger men as brothers, [2]older women
    as mothers, and younger women as sisters, with absolute
    purity.* (1 Timothy 5:1–2 NIV)

The _____ *of God*

In contrast to the Old Testament period in which Israel had a temple
(Exodus 25:8), the church is a temple: a living, vital temple.

¹⁹Consequently, you are no longer foreigners and aliens, but fellow citizens with God's people and members of God's household, ²⁰built on the foundation of the apostles and prophets, with Christ Jesus himself as the chief cornerstone. ²¹In him the whole building is joined together and rises to become a holy temple in the Lord. ²²And in him you too are being built together to become a dwelling in which God lives by his Spirit. (Ephesians 2:19–22 NIV)

- Jesus is pictured as the _____ .

- Individual believers are pictured as _____ .

⁴As you come to him, the living Stone—rejected by men but chosen by God and precious to him—⁵you also, like living stones, are being built into a spiritual house to be a holy priesthood, offering spiritual sacrifices acceptable to God through Jesus Christ. (1 Peter 2:4–5 NIV)

The _____ of Christ

- Israel was often portrayed in the Old Testament as being the

  _____ or _____ of God.

¹⁹And I will make you my promised bride forever. I will be good and fair; I will show you my love and mercy. ²⁰I will be true to you as my promised bride, and you will know the Lord. (Hosea 2:19–20 NCV)

- Israel was repeatedly _____ to her vows of love to God.

⁶This message from the Lord came to me during the reign of King Josiah: Have you seen what Israel does? Like a wanton wife who gives herself to other men at every chance, so Israel has worshiped other gods on every hill, beneath every shady tree. ⁷I thought that someday she would return to me and once again be mine; but she didn't come back. And her faithless sister Judah saw the continued rebellion of Israel. (Jeremiah 3:6–7 LB)

- The church is portrayed as being a _____ .

> *I am jealous for you with a godly jealousy. I promised you to one husband, to Christ, so that I might present you as a pure virgin to him.* (2 Corinthians 11:2 NIV)

The nature of the church

In Ephesians 5:22–33, the analogy is drawn comparing the husband-and-wife relationship in marriage to Christ and his bride, the church. The illustration is powerful because it reveals the magnitude of Christ's love for his church. He loved her enough to die for her. It also reveals the obedient response the church is to have to the bridegroom, Jesus Christ.

> *[25]Husbands, love your wives, just as Christ loved the church and gave himself up for her [26]to make her holy, cleansing her by the washing with water through the word.*
> (Ephesians 5:25–26 NIV)

1. The church lives with a sense of urgency to always be

   _____ for the Bridegroom.

> *[1]"At that time the kingdom of heaven will be like ten virgins who took their lamps and went out to meet the bridegroom. [2]Five of them were foolish and five were wise. [3]The foolish ones took their lamps but did not take any oil with them. [4]The wise, however, took oil in jars along with their lamps. [5]The bridegroom was a long time in coming, and they all became drowsy and fell asleep. [6]At midnight the cry rang out: 'Here's the bridegroom! Come out to meet him!' [7]Then all the virgins woke up and trimmed their lamps. [8]The foolish ones said to the wise, 'Give us some of your oil; our lamps are going out.' [9]'No,' they replied, 'there may not be enough for both us and you. Instead, go to those who sell oil and buy some for yourselves.' [10]But while they were on their way to buy the oil, the bridegroom arrived. The virgins who were ready went in with him to the wedding banquet. And the door was shut. [11]Later the others also came. 'Sir! Sir!' they said. 'Open the door for us!' [12]But he replied, 'I tell you the truth, I don't know you.' [13]Therefore keep watch, because you do not know the day or the hour."* (Matthew 25:1–13 NIV)

2. The church is to _____ others into the new relationship with the Bridegroom.

> [8] *"Then he said to his servants, 'The wedding banquet is ready, but those I invited did not deserve to come. [9]Go to the street corners and invite to the banquet anyone you find.'"*
> (Matthew 22:8–9 NIV)

Is the church of God a useless, worn-out institution? It doesn't have to be. God has made all the provisions necessary for local churches to be vibrant, transformational groups of believers who live interdependent, authentic lives of ministry and mission, building bridges so that lost people can find hope in God. The Devil can't stop us; the pervasive culture around us can't stop us. We are the only ones who can cause the church to lose its place of importance by not acting like the body of Christ, the flock of God, the family of God, the building of God, and the bride of Christ.

> *". . . I will build my church, and the gates of Hades will not overcome it."* (Matthew 16:18 NIV)

DISCOVERY QUESTIONS

1. How do you think believers' relationships should look different from the relationships of unbelievers? Why is Jesus' model often difficult for us to follow? What can help you grow to be more like Jesus in the way you treat others?

2. How does Peter's affirmation in 1 Peter 2:5 that we are like living stones help you understand your role within the church? How well do you recognize your need to depend on others?

3. *The church is the family of God.* How does this family concept help you picture your responsibilities toward other believers?

4. *The church is the building of God.* If you struggle with accepting believers from other denominations and churches as being "real" Christians, how does this truth help? Have you been trying to carry all of the weight of the Christian life on your shoulders? Where do you need to see the importance of your place in God's building? How can you recognize your dependence on others in the body of Christ? How could your group help you?

5. *The church is the bride of Christ.* Is there submission in your heart to Jesus as your Bridegroom? What priorities do you need to rearrange so that you can concentrate more on loving him?

Did You Get It? How has this week's study helped you see the significance and personal meaning of the church as the family of God, the building of God, and the bride of Christ?

Share with Someone: Think of a person you can encourage with the truth you learned in this session. Write their name in the space below and pray for God to provide that opportunity this week

LIVING ON PURPOSE
Fellowship and Worship

Share the Lord's Supper together. (Instructions for taking the Lord's Supper can be found in the Small Group Resources section, under *Serving the Lord's Supper,* pages 49–50.) As you begin, consider for a minute a bride and groom's feelings toward one another on their wedding day. Then liken it to your own relationship with Christ. Is there submission in your heart to Jesus as your Bridegroom? Take a couple of minutes to draw close to him in prayer as preparation for this time of communion.

PRAYER DIRECTION

Pray for other churches around the world. Pray for churches in countries where the number of believers is exploding. Pray for churches in countries where the church seems to be declining and dying. Especially pray for churches in countries where they are suffering persecution. (Go to www.opendoorsusa.org to get specific prayer requests for the persecuted church.)

NOTES

Small Group Resources

HELPS FOR HOSTS

Top Ten Ideas for New Hosts

Congratulations! As the host of your small group, you have responded to the call to help shepherd Jesus' flock. Few other tasks in the family of God surpass the contribution you will be making.

As you prepare to facilitate your group, whether it is one session or the entire series, here are a few thoughts to keep in mind. We encourage you to read and review these tips with each new discussion host before he or she leads.

Remember you are not alone. God knows everything about you, and he knew you would be asked to facilitate your group. Even though you may not feel ready, this is common for all good hosts. God promises, *"I will never leave you; I will never abandon you"* (Hebrews 13:5 TEV). Whether you are facilitating for one evening, several weeks, or a lifetime, you will be blessed as you serve.

1. **Don't try to do it alone.** Pray right now for God to help you build a healthy team. If you can enlist a cohost to help you shepherd the group, you will find your experience much richer. This is your chance to involve as many people as you can in building a healthy group. All you have to do is ask people to help. You'll be surprised at the response.

2. **Be friendly and be yourself.** God wants to use your unique gifts and temperament. Be sure to greet people at the door with a big smile . . . this can set the mood for the whole gathering. Remember, they are taking as big a step to show up at your house as you are to lead this group! Don't try to do things exactly like another host; do them in a way that fits you. Admit when you don't have an answer and apologize when you make a mistake. Your group will love you for it and you'll sleep better at night.

3. **Prepare for your meeting ahead of time.** Review the session and write down your responses to each question. Pay special attention to exercises that ask group members to do something other than engage in discussion. These exercises will help your group live what the Bible teaches, not just talk about it. Be sure you understand how an exercise works. If the exercise employs one of the items in the Small Group Resources section (such as the Group Guidelines), be sure to look over that item so you'll know how it works.

4. **Pray for your group members by name.** Before you begin your session, take a few moments and pray for each member by name. You may want to review the prayer list at least once a week. Ask God to use your time together to touch the heart of every person in your group. Expect God to lead you to whomever he wants you to encourage or challenge in a special way. If you listen, God will surely lead.

5. **When you ask a question, be patient.** Someone will eventually respond. Sometimes people need a moment or two of silence to think about the question. If silence doesn't bother you, it won't bother anyone else. After someone responds, affirm the response with a simple "thanks" or "great answer." Then ask, "How about somebody else?" or "Would someone who hasn't shared like to add anything?" Be sensitive to new people or reluctant members who aren't ready to say, pray, or do anything. If you give them a safe setting, they will blossom over time. If someone in your group is a "wallflower" who sits silently through every session, consider talking to them privately and encouraging them to participate. Let them know how important they are to you—that they are loved and appreciated—and that the group would value their input. Remember, still water often runs deep.

6. **Provide transitions between questions.** Ask if anyone would like to read the paragraph or Bible passage. Don't call on anyone, but ask for a volunteer, and then be patient until someone begins. Be sure to thank the person who reads aloud.

7. **Break into smaller groups occasionally.** With a greater opportunity to talk in a small circle, people will connect more with the study, apply more quickly what they're learning, and ultimately get more out of their small group experience. A small circle also encourages a quiet person to participate and tends to minimize the effects of a more vocal or dominant member.

8. **Small circles are also helpful during prayer time.** People who are unaccustomed to praying aloud will feel more comfortable trying it with just two or three others. Also, prayer requests won't take as much time, so circles will have more time to actually pray. When you gather back with the whole group, you can have one person from each circle briefly update everyone on the prayer requests from their subgroups. The other great aspect of subgrouping is that it fosters leadership development. As you ask people in the group to facilitate discussion or to lead a prayer circle, it gives them a small leadership step that can build their confidence.

9. **Rotate facilitators occasionally.** You may be perfectly capable of hosting each time, but you will help others grow in their faith and gifts if you give them opportunities to host the group.

10. **One final challenge (for new or first-time hosts).** Before your first opportunity to lead, look up each of the six passages that follow. Read each one as a devotional exercise to help prepare you with a shepherd's heart. Trust us on this one. If you do this, you will be more than ready for your first meeting.

Matthew 9:36–38 (NIV)
36When Jesus saw the crowds, he had compassion on them, because they were harassed and helpless, like sheep without a shepherd. 37Then he said to his disciples, "The harvest is plentiful but the workers are few. 38Ask the Lord of the harvest, therefore, to send out workers into his harvest field."

John 10:14–15 (NIV)
14I am the good shepherd; I know my sheep and my sheep know me—15just as the Father knows me and I know the Father—and I lay down my life for the sheep.

1 Peter 5:2–4 (NIV)

²Be shepherds of God's flock that is under your care, serving as overseers—not because you must, but because you are willing, as God wants you to be; ³not greedy for money, but eager to serve; not lording it over those entrusted to you, but being examples to the flock. ⁴And when the Chief Shepherd appears, you will receive the crown of glory that will never fade away.

Philippians 2:1–5 (NIV)

¹If you have any encouragement from being united with Christ, if any comfort from his love, if any fellowship with the Spirit, if any tenderness and compassion, ²then make my joy complete by being like-minded, having the same love, being one in spirit and purpose. ³Do nothing out of selfish ambition or vain conceit, but in humility consider others better than yourselves. ⁴Each of you should look not only to your own interests, but also to the interests of others. ⁵Your attitude should be the same as that of Jesus Christ.

Hebrews 10:23–25 (NIV)

²³Let us hold unswervingly to the hope we profess, for he who promised is faithful. ²⁴And let us consider how we may spur one another on toward love and good deeds. ²⁵Let us not give up meeting together, as some are in the habit of doing, but let us encourage one another—and all the more as you see the Day approaching.

1 Thessalonians 2:7–8, 11–12 (NIV)

⁷. . . but we were gentle among you, like a mother caring for her little children. ⁸We loved you so much that we were delighted to share with you not only the gospel of God but our lives as well, because you had become so dear to us. . . . ¹¹For you know that we dealt with each of you as a father deals with his own children, ¹²encouraging, comforting and urging you to live lives worthy of God, who calls you into his kingdom and glory.

FREQUENTLY ASKED QUESTIONS

How long will this group meet?

This volume of *Foundations: The Church* is four sessions long. We encourage your group to add a fifth session for a celebration. In your final session, each group member may decide if he or she desires to continue on for another study. At that time you may also want to do some informal evaluation, discuss your Group Guidelines, and decide which study you want to do next. We recommend you visit our website at **www.saddlebackresources.com** for more video-based small group studies.

Who is the host?

The host is the person who coordinates and facilitates your group meetings. In addition to a host, we encourage you to select one or more group members to lead your group discussions. Several other responsibilities can be rotated, including refreshments, prayer requests, worship, or keeping up with those who miss a meeting. Shared ownership in the group helps everybody grow.

Where do we find new group members?

Recruiting new members can be a challenge for groups, especially new groups with just a few people, or existing groups that lose a few people along the way. We encourage you to use the *Circles of Life* diagram on page 44 of this DVD study guide to brainstorm a list of people from your workplace, church, school, neighborhood, family, and so on. Then pray for the people on each member's list. Allow each member to invite several people from their list. Some groups fear that newcomers will interrupt the intimacy that members have built over time. However, groups that welcome newcomers generally gain strength with the infusion of new blood. Remember, the next person you add just might become a friend for eternity. Logistically, groups find different ways to add members. Some groups remain permanently open, while others choose to open periodically, such as at the beginning or end of a study. If your group becomes too large for easy, face-to-face conversations, you can subgroup, forming a second discussion group in another room.

How do we handle the child care needs in our group?

Child care needs must be handled very carefully. This is a sensitive issue. We suggest you seek creative solutions as a group. One common solution is to have the adults meet in the living room and share the cost of a babysitter (or two) who can be with the kids in another part of the house. Another popular option is to have one home for the kids and a second home (close by) for the adults. If desired, the adults could rotate the responsibility of providing a lesson for the kids. This last option is great with school-age kids and can be a huge blessing to families.

GROUP GUIDELINES

It's a good idea for every group to put words to their shared values, expectations, and commitments. Such guidelines will help you avoid unspoken agendas and unmet expectations. We recommend you discuss your guidelines during Session One in order to lay the foundation for a healthy group experience. Feel free to modify anything that does not work for your group.

We agree to the following values:

Clear Purpose　To grow healthy spiritual lives by building a healthy small group community

Group Attendance　To give priority to the group meeting (call if I am absent or late)

Safe Environment　To create a safe place where people can be heard and feel loved (no quick answers, snap judgments, or simple fixes)

Be Confidential　To keep anything that is shared strictly confidential and within the group

Conflict Resolution　To avoid gossip and to immediately resolve any concerns by following the principles of Matthew 18:15–17

Spiritual Health　To give group members permission to speak into my life and help me live a healthy, balanced spiritual life that is pleasing to God

Limit Our Freedom　To limit our freedom by not serving or consuming alcohol during small group meetings or events so as to avoid causing a weaker brother or sister to stumble (1 Corinthians 8:1–13; Romans 14:19–21)

Welcome Newcomers   To invite friends who might benefit from this study and warmly welcome newcomers

Building Relationships   To get to know the other members of the group and pray for them regularly

Other   _____

We have also discussed and agreed on the following items:

Child Care

_____

_____

Starting Time

_____

Ending Time

_____

If you haven't already done so, take a few minutes to fill out the *Small Group Calendar* on page 48.

CIRCLES OF LIFE—SMALL GROUP CONNECTIONS

Discover who you can connect in community

Use this chart to help carry out one of the values in the Group Guidelines, to "Welcome Newcomers."

"Follow me, and I will make you fishers of men." (Matthew 4:19 KJV)

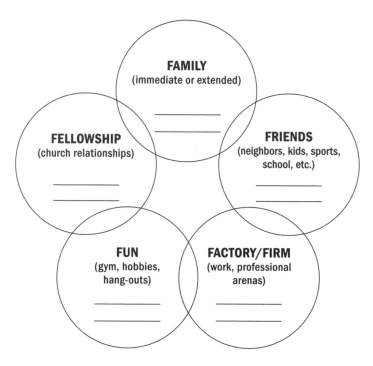

Follow this simple three-step process:

1. List 1–2 people in each circle.

2. Prayerfully select one person or couple from your list and tell your group about them.

3. Give them a call and invite them to your next meeting. Over 50 percent of those invited to a small group say, "Yes!"

SMALL GROUP PRAYER AND PRAISE REPORT

This is a place where you can write each other's requests for prayer. You can also make a note when God answers a prayer. Pray for each other's requests. If you're new to group prayer, it's okay to pray silently or to pray by using just one sentence: "God, please help

_____ to _____ ."

DATE	PERSON	PRAYER REQUEST	PRAISE REPORT

SMALL GROUP PRAYER AND PRAISE REPORT

DATE	PERSON	PRAYER REQUEST	PRAISE REPORT

SMALL GROUP PRAYER AND PRAISE REPORT

DATE	PERSON	PRAYER REQUEST	PRAISE REPORT

SMALL GROUP CALENDAR

Healthy groups share responsibilities and group ownership. It might take some time for this to develop. Shared ownership ensures that responsibility for the group doesn't fall to one person. Use the calendar to keep track of social events, mission projects, birthdays, or days off. Complete this calendar at your first or second meeting. Planning ahead will increase attendance and shared ownership.

DATE	LESSON	LOCATION	FACILITATOR	SNACK OR MEAL
5/4	Session 2	Chris and Andrea	Jim Brown	Phil and Karen

SERVING THE LORD'S SUPPER

[23] . . . The Lord Jesus, on the night he was betrayed, took bread, [24] and when he had given thanks, he broke it and said, "This is my body, which is for you; do this in remembrance of me." [25] In the same way, after supper he took the cup, saying, "This cup is the new covenant in my blood; do this, whenever you drink it, in remembrance of me." [26] For whenever you eat this bread and drink this cup, you proclaim the Lord's death until he comes. (1 Corinthians 11:23–26 NIV)

Steps in Serving Communion

(Before serving communion in your small group, check with your pastor and church leadership to be sure that serving communion in a small group fits the practice and philosophy of your church.)

1. Open by sharing about God's love, forgiveness, grace, mercy, commitment, tenderheartedness, faithfulness, etc., out of your personal journey (connect with stories of those in the room).

2. Read the passage: *. . . The Lord Jesus, on the night he was betrayed, took bread, and when he had given thanks, he broke it and said, "This is my body, which is for you; do this in remembrance of me."* (vv. 23–24)

3. Pray and pass the bread around the circle (this could be time for quiet reflection, singing a simple praise song, or listening to a worship CD).

4. When everyone has been served, remind him or her that this represents Jesus' body broken on their behalf. Simply state, "Jesus said, *'Do this in remembrance of me.'* Let us eat together," and eat the bread as a group.

5. Then read the rest of the passage: *In the same way, after supper he took the cup, saying, "This cup is the new covenant in my blood; do this, whenever you drink it, in remembrance of me."* (v. 25)

6. Pray and serve the cups, either by passing a small tray, serving them individually, or having members pick up a cup from the table.

7. When everyone has been served, remind them the juice represents Christ's blood shed for them, then simply state, "Take and drink in remembrance of him. Let us drink together."

8. Finish by singing a simple song, listening to a praise song, or having a time of prayer in thanks to God.

Several Practical Tips in Serving Communion

1. Be sensitive to timing in your meeting.

2. Break up pieces of cracker or soft bread on a small plate or tray. Don't use large servings of bread or juice.

3. Prepare all of the elements beforehand and bring these into the room when you are ready.

Communion passages: Matthew 26:26–29; Mark 14:22–25; Luke 22:14–20; 1 Corinthians 10:16–21, 11:17–34

ANSWER KEY

Session One:
How the Church Began

1. Envisioned by God
2. Established by Jesus
3. Energized by the Spirit

The church is an ekklesia.

Ekklesia refers to both the universal church and the local church.

- In the universal church the emphasis is on the unity of the church.
- In the local church the emphasis is on the ministry of the church.

The church is a koinonia.

1. Light
2. Unity
3. Acceptance
4. Sharing of material goods
5. Giving money
6. Suffering
7. Lord's Supper

Session Two:
The Purpose of the Church

1. "Love God with all your heart": worship
2. "Love your neighbor as yourself": ministry
3. "Go and make disciples": evangelism
4. "Baptizing them": fellowship
5. "Teaching them to do": discipleship

1. Celebrate God's presence
2. Communicate God's Word
3. Incorporate God's family
4. Educate God's people
5. Demonstrate God's love

Session Three:
Metaphors for the Church

The body of Christ

1) unity
2) diversity

- Christ breaking down the wall of separation
- Our oneness in Christ's body
- Our equal standing at the cross
- A common citizenship, a common family, and a common future destination

The wrong way: gossip

The right way: confront it

The flock of God

- We are the sheep.
- Jesus is the shepherd.

Session Four:
Metaphors for the Church—Part 2

The family (household) of God

- God adopts us into his family.
- We're to treat one another as family.

The building of God

- Jesus is pictured as the chief cornerstone.
- Individual believers are pictured as living stones.

The bride of Christ

- Israel was often portrayed in the Old Testament as being the wife or bride of God.
- Israel was repeatedly unfaithful to her vows of love to God.
- The church is portrayed as being a virgin bride.

1. The church lives with a sense of urgency to always be prepared for the Bridegroom.
2. The church is to invite others into the new relationship with the Bridegroom.

NOTES

KEY VERSES

One of the most effective ways to drive deeply into our lives the principles we are learning in this series is to memorize key Scriptures. For many, memorization is a new concept or one that has been difficult in the past. We encourage you to stretch yourself and try to memorize these four key verses. If possible, memorize these as a group and make them part of your group time. You may cut these apart and carry them in your wallet.

I have hidden your word in my heart that I might not sin against you.

Psalm 119:11 (NIV)

Session One

"And I tell you that you are Peter, and on this rock I will build my church, and the gates of Hades will not overcome it."

Matthew 16:18 (NIV)

Session Two

Let us not give up meeting together, as some are in the habit of doing, but let us encourage one another— and all the more as you see the Day approaching.

Hebrews 10:25 (NIV)

Session Three

Now you are no longer strangers to God and foreigners to heaven, but you are members of God's very own family, citizens of God's country, and you belong in God's household with every other Christian.

Ephesians 2:19 (LB)

Session Four

For we were all baptized by one Spirit into one body—whether Jews or Greeks, slave or free—and we were all given the one Spirit to drink.

1 Corinthians 12:13 (NIV)

NOTES

We value your thoughts about what you've just read.
Please share them with us. You'll find contact information
in the back of this book.

The Purpose Driven® Life
A six-session video-based study for groups or individuals

Embark on a journey of discovery with this video-based study taught by Rick Warren. In it you will discover the answer to life's most fundamental question: "What on earth am I here for?"

And here's a clue to the answer: "It's not about you . . . You were created by God and for God, and until you understand that, life will never make sense. It is only in God that we discover our origin, our identity, our meaning, our purpose, our significance, and our destiny."

Whether you experience this adventure with a small group or on your own, this six-session, video-based study will change your life.

DVD Study Guide: 978-0-310-27866-5
DVD: 978-0-310-27864-1

Be sure to combine this study with your reading of the best-selling book, *The Purpose Driven® Life*, to give you or your small group the opportunity to discuss the implications and applications of living the life God created you to live.

Hardcover, Jacketed: 978-0-310-20571-5
Softcover: 978-0-310-27699-9

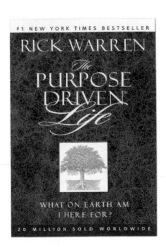

Pick up a copy today at your favorite bookstore!

Foundations: 11 Core Truths to Build Your Life On

Taught by Tom Holladay and Kay Warren

Foundations is a series of 11 four-week video studies covering the most important, foundational doctrines of the Christian faith. Study topics include:

The Bible—This study focuses on where the Bible came from, why it can be trusted, and how it can change your life.
DVD Study Guide: 978-0-310-27670-8
DVD: 978-0-310-27669-2

God—This study focuses not just on facts about God, but on how to know God himself in a more powerful and personal way.
DVD Study Guide: 978-0-310-27672-2
DVD: 978-0-310-27671-5

Jesus—As we look at what the Bible says about the person of Christ, we do so as people who are developing a lifelong relationship with Jesus.
DVD Study Guide: 978-0-310-27674-6
DVD: 978-0-310-27673-9

The Holy Spirit—This study focuses on the person, the presence, and the power of the Holy Spirit, and how you can be filled with the Holy Spirit on a daily basis.
DVD Study Guide: 978-0-310-27676-0
DVD: 978-0-310-27675-3

Creation—Each of us was personally created by a loving God. This study does not shy away from the great scientific and theological arguments that surround the creation/evolution debate. However, you will find the goal of this study is deepening your awareness of God as your Creator.
DVD Study Guide: 978-0-310-27678-4
DVD: 978-0-310-27677-7

Pick up a copy today at your favorite bookstore!

ZONDERVAN®
.com

Salvation—This study focuses on God's solution to man's need for salvation, what Jesus Christ did for us on the cross, and the assurance and security of God's love and provision for eternity.

DVD Study Guide: 978-0-310-27682-1
DVD: 978-0-310-27679-1

Sanctification—This study focuses on the two natures of the Christian. We'll see the difference between grace and law, and how these two things work in our lives.

DVD Study Guide: 978-0-310-27684-5
DVD: 978-0-310-27683-8

Good and Evil—Why do bad things happen to good people? Through this study we'll see how and why God continues to allow evil to exist. The ultimate goal is to build up our faith and relationship with God as we wrestle with these difficult questions.

DVD Study Guide: 978-0-310-27687-6
DVD: 978-0-310-27686-9

The Afterlife—The Bible does not answer all the questions we have about what happens to us after we die; however, this study deals with what the Bible does tell us. This important study gives us hope and helps us move from a focus on the here and now to a focus on eternity.

DVD Study Guide: 978-0-310-27689-0
DVD: 978-0-310-27688-3

The Church—This study focuses on the birth of the church, the nature of the church, and the mission of the church.

DVD Study Guide: 978-0-310-27692-0
DVD: 978-0-310-27691-3

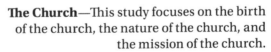

The Second Coming—This study addresses both the hope and the uncertainties surrounding the second coming of Jesus Christ.

DVD Study Guide: 978-0-310-27695-1
DVD: 978-0-310-27693-7

Pick up a copy today at your favorite bookstore!

ZONDERVAN®
.com

Celebrate Recovery, Updated Curriculum Kit

This kit will provide your church with the tools necessary to start a successful Celebrate Recovery program. *Kit includes:*

- Introductory Guide for Leaders DVD
- Leader's Guide
- 4 Participant's Guides (one of each guide)
- CD-ROM with 25 lessons
- CD-ROM with sermon transcripts
- 4-volume audio CD sermon series

Curriculum Kit: 978-0-310-26847-5

Participant's Guide 4-pack

The Celebrate Recovery Participant's Guide 4-pack is a convenient resource when you're just getting started or if you need replacement guides for your program.

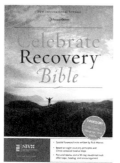

Celebrate Recovery Bible

With features based on eight principles Jesus voiced in his Sermon on the Mount, the new *Celebrate Recovery Bible* offers hope, encouragement, and empowerment for those struggling with the circumstances of their lives and the habits they are trying to control.

Hardcover: 978-0-310-92849-2
Softcover: 978-0-310-93810-1

Pick up a copy today at your favorite bookstore!

ZONDERVAN®
.com

Stepping Out of Denial into God's Grace

Participant's Guide 1 introduces the eight principles of recovery based on Jesus' words in the Beatitudes, and focuses on principles 1–3. Participants learn about denial, hope, sanity, and more.

Getting Right with God, Yourself, and Others

Participant's Guide 3 covers principles 5–7 based on Jesus' words in the Beatitudes. With courage and support from their fellow participants, people seeking recovery will find victory, forgiveness, and grace.

Taking an Honest and Spiritual Inventory

Participant's Guide 2 focuses on the fourth principle based on Jesus' words in the Beatitudes and builds on the Scripture, *"Happy are the pure in heart."* (Matthew 5:8) The participant will learn an invaluable principle for recovery and also take an in-depth spiritual inventory.

Growing in Christ While Helping Others

Participant's Guide 4 walks through the final steps of the eight recovery principles based on Jesus' words in the Beatitudes. In this final phase, participants learn to move forward in newfound freedom in Christ, learning how to give back to others. There's even a practical lesson called "Seven reasons we get stuck in our recoveries."

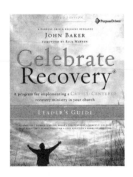

Leader's Guide

The Celebrate Recovery Leader's Guide gives you everything you need to facilitate your preparation time. Virtually walking you through every meeting, the Leader's Guide is a must-have for every leader on your Celebrate Recovery ministry team.

Pick up a copy today at your favorite bookstore!

ZONDERVAN®
.com

Wide Angle: Framing Your Worldview

Christianity is much more than a religion. It is a worldview—a way of seeing all of life and the world around you. Your worldview impacts virtually every decision you make in life: moral decisions, relational decisions, financial decisions—everything. How you see the world determines how you face the world.

In this brand new study, Rick Warren and Chuck Colson discuss such key issues as moral relativism, tolerance, terrorism, creationism vs. Darwinism, sin and suffering. They explore in depth the Christian worldview as it relates to the most important questions in life:

- Why does it matter what I believe?
- How do I know what's true?
- Where do I come from?
- Why is the world so messed up?
- Is there a solution?
- What is my purpose in life?

This study is as deep as it is wide, addressing vitally important topics for every follower of Christ.

DVD Study Guide: 978-1-4228-0083-6
DVD: 978-1-4228-0082-9

Rick Warren

Chuck Colson

The Way of a Worshiper

The pursuit of God is the chase of a lifetime—in fact, it's been going on since the day you were born. The question is: Have you been the hunter or the prey?

This small group study is not about music. It's not even about going to church. It's about living your life as an offering of worship to God. It's about tapping into the source of power to live the Christian life. And it's about discovering the secret to friendship with God.

In these four video sessions, Buddy Owens helps you unpack the meaning of worship. Through his very practical, engaging, and at times surprising insights, Buddy shares truths from Scripture and from life that will help you understand in a new and deeper way just what it means to be a worshiper.

God is looking for worshipers. His invitation to friendship is open and genuine. Will you take him up on his offer? Will you give yourself to him in worship? Then come walk *The Way of a Worshiper* and discover the secret to friendship with God.

DVD Study Guide: 978-1-4228-0096-6
DVD: 978-1-4228-0095-9

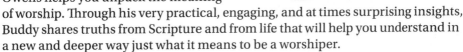

THE WAY of a WORSHIPER

Your study of this material will be greatly enhanced by reading the book, *The Way of a Worshiper: Discover the Secret to Friendship with God.*

Managing Our Finances God's Way

Did you know that there are over 2,350 verses in the Bible about money? Did you know that nearly half of Jesus' parables are about possessions? The Bible is packed with wise counsel about your financial life. In fact, Jesus had more to say about money than about heaven and hell combined.

Introducing a new video-based small group study that will inspire you to live debt free! Created by Saddleback Church and Crown Financial Ministries, learn what the Bible has to say about our finances from Rick Warren, Chip Ingram, Ron Blue, Howard Dayton, and Chuck Bentley as they address important topics like:

- God's Solution to Debt
- Saving and Investing
- Plan Your Spending
- Giving as an Act of Worship
- Enjoy What God Has Given You

Study includes:

- DVD with seven 20-minute lessons

- Workbook with seven lessons

- Resource CD with digital version of all worksheets that perform calculations automatically

- Contact information for help with answering questions

- Resources for keeping financial plans on track and making them lifelong habits

NOTE: PARTICIPANTS DO NOT SHARE PERSONAL FINANCIAL INFORMATION WITH EACH OTHER.

DVD Study Guide: 978-1-4228-0083-6
DVD: 978-1-4228-0082-9

Share Your Thoughts

With the Author: Your comments will be forwarded to
the author when you send them to *zauthor@zondervan.com*.

With Zondervan: Submit your review of this book
by writing to *zreview@zondervan.com*.

Free Online Resources at

www.zondervan.com/hello

 Zondervan AuthorTracker: Be notified whenever your favorite authors publish new books, go on tour, or post an update about what's happening in their lives.

 Daily Bible Verses and Devotions: Enrich your life with daily Bible verses or devotions that help you start every morning focused on God.

 Free Email Publications: Sign up for newsletters on fiction, Christian living, church ministry, parenting, and more.

 Zondervan Bible Search: Find and compare Bible passages in a variety of translations at www.zondervanbiblesearch.com.

 Other Benefits: Register yourself to receive online benefits like coupons and special offers, or to participate in research.